GREAT PETS

Frogs

Johannah Haney

Marshall Cavendish
Benchmark
New York

Marshall Cavendish Benchmark
99 White Plains Road
Tarrytown, New York 10591
www.marshallcavendish.us

All websites were available and accurate when this book was sent to press.

Library of Congress Cataloging-in-Publication Data
Haney, Johannah.
Frogs / by Johannah Haney.
p. cm. -- (Great pets)
"Describes the characteristics and behavior of pet frogs, also discussing their physical appearance and place in history"--Provided by publisher.
Includes bibliographical references and index.
ISBN 978-0-7614-4151-9
1. Frogs as pets--Juvenile literature. I. Title.
SF459.F83H36 2009
639.3'789--dc22
2008037242

Front cover: A tree frog
Back cover: An aquatic dwarf frog
Photo Research by Candlepants Incorporated
Front cover: Gail Shumway / Getty
The photographs in this book are used by permission and through the courtesy of:
Getty: Grank Greenaway, 1; Robin Smith, 4; Jerry Young, 14; Stephen Cooper, 19; Joe McDonald, 23; Gerold & Cynthia Merker, 24; Gail Shumway, 27; Ken Lucas, 28; Robert Lindholm, 29; Geoff Brightling, 30, 41; Burke/Triolog Productions, 43. Alamy: Maximilian Weinzierl, 8; A&P, 13, back cover; Christine Strover, 16; Ridley - Stock, 20; Steve Hamblin, 22; fotototo, 25; Hans-Peter Moehlig, 34; blickwinkel, 37; JUPITERIMAGES / Brand X, 40.Animals Animals - Earth Scenes: Lightwave Photography, 21; Leszczynski, Zigmund, 33. AP: Gary Kazanjian, 38. Corbis: Lebrecht Music & Arts, 6. Peter Arnold: Biosphoto / Gunther Michel, 10; Biosphoto / Noblet Jean-Francois, 32. Mingei International Museum / Art Resource. NY: 7.

Editor: Karen Ang
Publisher: Michelle Bisson
Art Director: Anahid Hamparian
Series Designer: Elynn Cohen

Printed in Malaysia
1 3 5 6 4 2

Contents

1

Frog Facts

In many ancient myths, frogs represent **fertility** and renewal. Ancient Egyptians worshiped Heqet—a woman with the head of a frog—as the goddess of fertility and childbirth. Chan Chu is a Chinese symbol of prosperity. Chan Chu means "Money Frog" and it is supposed to ward off evil and bring good luck and wealth. In the native Aymara cultures of Peru and Bolivia, frogs, called *K'aira,* are an important symbol for rain.

Modern-day fairy tales sometimes use frogs as central characters. One of the most famous examples is *The Frog Prince,* a Brothers-Grimm fairy tale, in which a beautiful princess who is searching for her prince meets a frog. In modern versions of the story, the princess kisses the frog and it turns into her handsome prince. Other frog figures in popular culture are *Sesame*

Frogs hatch from eggs, start out as tadpoles that spend all of their time in the water, and then develop into frogs that can live on land and water.

The Frog Prince is one of the most famous stories involving a frog and how it changes forms during its lifetime.

Street's Kermit the Frog; Jeremy Fisher, from Beatrix Potter's books; and Frog from Arnold Lobel's *Frog and Toad* books.

Today there are more than five thousand different species of frogs, each with different characteristics that make it unique. Gardiner's Seychelles frog is the smallest species. It is just half an inch long. The goliath frog, on the other hand, is the largest frog on earth. It can grow to be 12 inches long and weigh up to 8 pounds! The common wood frog, which lives in the far northern Americas, freezes solid in the winter, then thaws when the temperature warms up. Not all frog species make good pets, but there are some species that are perfect for interested pet owners.

Ancient cultures often made pottery that used frog shapes and symbols.

Frog Life

A frog begins as an egg floating in water. When it hatches it is a tadpole that lives completely underwater and breathes with its gills. It uses its tail to swim through the water since it does not have any legs. Over the course of several days to several weeks, the tadpole begins to change. Its gills disappear and lungs start to form. Lungs are the organs that most oxygen-breathing animals use to breathe air. The tadpole's tail starts to disappear and four legs start to stick out from its body. Soon it will be ready to live part of its life on land. This process of changing from a tadpole into a frog is known as **metamorphosis.**

Slimy Skin

Frog skin is permeable, which means that water, oxygen, and other chemicals can flow in and out. When they are in water, frogs can absorb oxygen through their skin. When they are on land, they breathe through their nostrils and have lungs, like many other animals. Because of this, frogs usually stay near water so they can stay moist. Their skin produces a special coating that acts as a barrier to prevent the frog from drying out. This is how frogs get their reputation for being slimy.

Most types of frogs shed their skin, or **molt.** This helps them keep their skin thin and healthy. Some frogs molt very frequently—some as often as every few days. Sometimes a molting frog pulls its old skin off and eats it.

A molting tree frog eats some of its shedded skin.

Pet Frogs

As with other pets, keeping a pet frog is a big responsibility. It can be expensive to buy a large **terrarium** with enough space to keep a frog happy. Frogs' terrariums must be kept clean and their water must be changed frequently. Many types of frogs must be fed live insects or animals, which can be difficult if you do not like to handle bugs and mice. Because of this, it can be difficult to find someone to care for your frog if you must go out of town. Some species of frogs are not very active, which can sometimes make them seem less interesting to some people.

However, having a pet frog can also be very rewarding. Pet frogs can live for several years. Caring for a frog as it grows and changes can be a fun learning experience.

Frog or Toad?

Whether you consider something a frog or a toad can depend on if you are a scientist or where you live. Scientists group frogs and toads into an animal category called Anura. All anurans are **amphibians.** An amphibian is a type of animal that lives partly in water, partly on land, and undergoes a major body change during its lifetime. Many scientists do not really separate most frogs and toads—to them they are all frogs. (However, some scientists refer to specific **species**, or types, of anurans as "true toads.")

Most people in North America and Europe consider frogs to be the smooth skinned, long-legged creatures that hop around. To them, toads are different and have rough and warty skin and shorter legs. In other parts of the world, many people do not even use the terms "frog" or "toad."

2

Frogs as Pets

Deciding which type of frog to keep as a pet is an important decision. Some types of frogs are very active, while others do not seem to move around a lot. Certain species can be kept with other frogs, or even fish, but others need to have their own terrariums. Depending on which species you choose, you might have to handle live insects or rodents to feed to your frog.

Before buying a frog you should do a lot of research. Find out which species are most commonly kept, and what kind of care they require. Will you need a lot of space? What kind of food do they eat? Will they grow very big? Do they make a lot of noise?

Not all frogs make good pets for everyone. This colorful poison dart frog is small and may seem easy and fun to care for, but it is actually a pet frog better suited to experienced frog owners. Careful research will help you pick the frog that is perfect for you.

Wild Frogs

You may encounter a frog on a walk in the woods or near a creek by your home. If you have been considering a pet frog, this might seem like the perfect solution. However, it is not a good idea to get a pet frog from the wild. Frogs in the wild may have a disease that you are unaware of, which is a concern especially if you have other frogs or toads. Since it can be difficult to identify which species a frog belongs to just by looking, you will not know what it eats, how much land area and water it needs, how big it will get, whether it is safe to keep with other pets, or how much space it needs.

Some states have laws that make it illegal to capture a wild frog for a pet. The type of frog you find could be an endangered species. Frogs that are endangered need to remain in the wild so they can reproduce to help keep the species alive. Buying your frog from a reliable pet store or **breeder** is the best way to get your new pet.

Where to Buy a Frog

There are a few different places to buy frogs, each with advantages and disadvantages. Many pet stores have frogs waiting for homes, and it can be a good place to go to pick out your new pet frog. However, not every pet store specializes in amphibians, so make sure you look for a frog that is healthy and kept in a clean environment.

No matter where you get your frog or what type you decide to get, it is important to examine how the frog is being kept and treated. Frogs of all ages and types should have a clean environment with plenty of room. If the terrariums at the pet store or breeder look small and dirty, do not buy your frog from there. Frogs kept in those conditions will most likely be sick.

Some pet stores that sell amphibians are more knowledgeable than others. Ask any questions you may have about where the frog came from and how to take care of it. If it seems like the store workers do not know the answers, you might consider going somewhere where they are more knowledgeable. Check where the frogs are being kept. Does the tank look clean? Do the frogs seem healthy and well fed?

Be sure to check all parts of your frog to make sure it is not sick and does not have any wounds. This includes checking its belly, its legs and its feet.

Throughout the United States, many people who are interested in amphibians and reptiles meet to sell animals and supplies. These shows can be a wonderful way to learn more about different pet frogs before buying one. Breeders who bring animals and supplies to the show can give you the information you need while also offering a bigger variety of amphibian supplies for your pet. Many of these events only allow the sale of captive-bred frogs, which means you are more likely to find a healthy pet that was not taken from the wild. Frogs that were born in captivity are less likely to have diseases than frogs captured in the wild. You can usually find information about amphibian and reptile shows on the Internet.

Healthy Frogs

When you are choosing which pet to bring home, look for signs of healthy frogs. A healthy frog should have clear, alert eyes and a healthy appetite. Make sure the skin is not broken and does not have unusual blisters, sores, or bumps. You should also look for any **fungus** growths on the frog's skin. This might look like white, gray, or yellow fluff, and can be a sign of disease or poorly cared for frogs. Healthy frogs of most species have a quick escape reflex. That means that when you try to touch the frog, it leaps away in a flash to avoid you. A frog that is too thin or slow will probably be unhealthy and might not make the best pet—especially if you already have other frogs at home.

3

Choosing a Frog

There are so many different species of frog, but only a few make good pets. Asking breeders, pet store workers, and researching pet frog species can help you choose the right amphibious friend.

Each species of frog has special needs you must learn about so you can take care of your new friend. Some frogs live underwater most of the time, while others need a land base. Some species of frogs are nocturnal, meaning they sleep during the day and are active at night. Certain frog species require special diets that may be very expensive or hard to find. Be sure you are able to provide these things before selecting a frog.

Toxic Frogs

Most frogs have special parts in their skin that contain **toxins,** or poison. Some toxins are strong enough to paralyze or kill **predators** instantly, but

Tree frogs are some of the most popular pet frogs. They are good for a first-time frog owner, but still require time and attention.

most are not that serious. These toxins might make them taste bad to potential predators. In humans, the toxins can be absorbed through the skin when they handle the frogs or the frogs' supplies. The toxins secreted, or let out, by most pet frogs do not cause death to humans, but can cause irritation and some illness. It is always important to wash your hands with soap and water after feeding or handling your frog and its terrarium. You should also be aware of whether or not your pet frog is a species that releases toxins.

White's Tree Frog

White's Tree Frogs are very popular pets. Females grow to be about 5 inches, and males are smaller—sometimes half the size of females. Most of these tree frogs are green. This species of frog is very popular because it is a good pet for a first-time frog owner. The frogs are content to sit quietly in their terrarium and do not require a lot of specialized care. Because they are nocturnal, these frogs tend to be more active at night. With proper care, White's Tree Frogs can live for ten years.

This tree frog's terrarium should have a dry area and fresh water. The water can be provided in a bowl that is deep enough for the frog to rest in, but not so deep or wide that it cannot get out. Though these frogs will often climb and stick to the sides of the terrarium, you should offer your frog hiding places and safe structures to climb and rest upon. You must also make sure that the terrarium has a cover so that your frog cannot escape.

Many people like keeping White's Tree Frogs because the frogs often look like they are smiling.

White's Tree Frogs eat small live food like crickets, worms, and sometimes tiny newborn mice. (These mice are called pinkies and are sold at pet stores and by certain amphibian and reptile breeders.) Because these frogs do not move around a lot, it is easy for them to become overweight.

Carefully feeding your frog the right amount of food will keep it healthier for a longer period of time. A frog breeder or a **veterinarian** can help you determine what the right amount of food is.

American Bullfrogs

In the wild, the American bullfrog is common to many parts of the United States, and is the largest frog in North America. Some American bullfrogs can grow to have 7-inch-long bodies. These green and brown frogs get their name from the sounds they make. Their croaks sound like the mooing of a bull.

Many frogs—including White's Tree Frogs—have special parts on their toes and feet that act like suction cups, allowing them to stick to the walls of their terrariums.

Because they are big, pet bullfrogs need a large, secure place to live. They need a terrarium that has a section with water that is deep enough to cover their bodies. Your bullfrog will also need a dry section. A pet bullfrog can be fed worms, crickets, and

Bullfrogs can come in a wide range of colors, from brown to green to a mix of colors and spots.

small mice. Because bullfrogs get big and will eat smaller animals, it is not a good idea to keep more than one bullfrog in the terrarium.

African Dwarf Frogs

African dwarf frogs live most of their lives underwater. They come to the surface for air every so often. They can grow to be 2 inches long, and can live for about five years. These frogs can be kept in a water-filled 10-gallon tank, and may be kept with certain fish. (The fish in the tank should not be small enough for the frog to eat and should be fish that are not likely to attack other animals.) These frogs can also live with other frogs of the same species.

Be careful when selecting an aquatic frog. Some species of African frogs are not dwarf and can grow to become very large.

African dwarf frogs are bottom feeders, which means they do not go to the surface of water to eat. These frogs can be fed brine shrimp, sinking food pellets, or bloodworms. All of these foods can be found at pet stores.

Some African dwarf frogs sold in large pet stores may have a fungus called Chytrid fungus. This illness can kill the frogs. Unfortunately, signs of the disease are not always visible. So if you are buying a new frog, keep it separate for a few weeks before introducing it to a tank with other fish or frogs.

Fire-Bellied Toads

Even though they are called toads, these frogs are very popular pets. A fire-bellied toad has splashes of vivid red or orange on its underside. In the wild, the color is used to scare away larger animals and prevent them from eating the frogs. Fire-bellied toads eat a diet of worms, crickets, and other insects.

Fire-bellied toads need a combination of water and land in their terrarium or tank. When picking out a tank, you should average about 5 gallons of space per frog. Because these frogs secrete a toxin through their skin, the water in their tanks must be changed at least once a week so the toxin does not build up and harm the animals. When properly cared for, these frogs can live for more than five years and grow to be about 1 to 3 inches long.

Like most frogs, fire-bellied toads have toxins in their skin. This should not be dangerous to humans as long as they wash their hands well after handling the frog and its terrarium.

Leopard frogs can be found in the wild, but pet leopard frogs should be captive bred and purchased from a store or a breeder.

Leopard Frogs

Leopard frogs grow to be 3 to 5 inches and are dotted with dark spots. The frog's name comes from its spots' resemblance to a leopard's spots. This species needs both land and water, and thrives in a terrarium that is 20 gallons or more. Adult frogs eat two to three insects at a time, and they feed every other day. Leopard frogs have a good appetite and will eat most types of insects. They will even eat smaller animals, so make sure you keep them separate from smaller frogs and fish.

Pacman Frogs

These frogs are actually Argentine horned frogs, but are often called Pacman frogs after the famous video game character. Like Pacman, these frogs have large mouths and stomachs. Males grow to be about 7 inches, and females grow to be about 9 inches. Because of their size, a tank that is at least 15 to 20 gallons is recommended. Pacman

A Pacman frog might try to eat just about anything it can fit into its mouth.

frogs are best housed alone because they are fierce predators and will try to eat smaller animals.

Pacman frogs eat crickets and small mice. You should be careful about feeding your Pacman frog since it can accidentally bite your fingers. Many Pacman frog owners use tongs to lower food into their pets' terrariums. This species lives to be about six years old in captivity, although some have been known to live longer.

Poison Dart Frogs

Poison dart frogs are some of the most brightly colored frogs. They are also some of the most poisonous. They get their common name from the fact that native people in South America dip their weapons in the poison from the frogs' skin. This helps them when hunting for larger animals. Like many poisonous animals, the frogs' bright colors are a warning to predators in the wild. Scientists have discovered that for many of these frogs, the poison comes from the toxins in food they eat in the wild. For that reason, some of these frogs are not poisonous in captivity.

Even though these frogs are very pretty, they are not ideal pets. Poison dart frogs are small—some are even only 1 inch long when fully grown. They have very specific diets of small bugs and need a terrarium with the right amount of water, light, and heat. These frogs are usually bought from special breeders and can be expensive.

Poison dart frogs come in a variety of colors. The more colorful ones are usually harder to find and more expensive.

The Most Poisonous Frog

The golden dart frog is believed to be Earth's most poisonous animal. This frog lives in the rainforests of western Colombia. Its skin secretes poison strong enough to kill 20,000 mice or eight to ten humans!

Frog Noises

Frogs have a variety of vocalizations, or sounds, that mean different things. Male frogs have a mating call they use to attract a female. In the wild, the louder and more booming the call, the more attractive it is to a female. Many species of frogs have a **vocal sac** under the chin or on both sides of their chins. This vocal sac helps make the sound of a frog's call louder and more attractive to females. Males also make specific sounds to establish their territory.

Both male and female frogs make distress calls and warning calls. Distress calls are high-pitched squeals or screams that a frog might use if it faces an immediate threat, like a predator. The call may startle the predator and give the frog a chance to leap to safety. Warning calls are used to communicate danger to other nearby frogs.

Not all frogs have vocal sacs that enlarge when they make noises. Your frog can still be a loud noisemaker even if it does not have large vocal sacs.

Your frog might make some noises during the day or at night. Usually, these noises are a normal part of their activities. Before choosing a pet frog, you should make sure that the species you choose is not too noisy. Some really noisy frogs have been known to keep their owners up at night!

4

Caring for Your Pet Frog

Bringing Your Pet Home

Your pet frog might be nervous as you are transporting it home. You can help it to stay calm—and healthy—by being prepared for its arrival. Most breeders or pet stores will give you a container in which to bring your frog home. However, sometimes you can bring your own. An empty plastic box with air holes and a secure lid can be used to transport your frog. (This can also be used later if you bring your frog to a veterinarian.)

Make sure its terrarium is set up in advance and stocked with fresh water so it can get to know its new home right away. Place the plastic box with your frog in its terrarium. If there is space, remove the lid, and let it leave the box on its own when it is ready. If there is not enough space,

With the proper care, your pet frog can be your companion for several years.

gently lower your frog into the terrarium. For the first day or two, leave the frog alone as much as possible to get comfortable in its new home.

Housing

Most pet owners keep their frogs in a terrarium that is set up to provide the right balance of land and water for the particular frog species. All frogs need an area of water to keep their skin moist. It is important that you keep this water fresh. If you use tap water, make sure you remove chlorine or other

The water you provide for your frog should be changed at least once a week.

A terrarium can have many different parts, but keep in mind that you will need to remove and clean everything whenever you clean the terrarium.

chemicals from the water by letting the water sit out for 24 hours before using it, or by using water treatments that remove chemicals. If your frog is an aquatic frog that stays in water all the time, then ask a veterinarian, breeder, or pet store worker how to set up a water tank.

Pet stores and breeders can suggest the right kind of material with which to fill the floor of your frog's terrarium.

Most frogs need an area where they can relax, hunt, and play on dry land. Coconut husk fiber is often a good choice in the dry land area because frogs can burrow in it, it holds moisture, and it will not harm your pet frog if swallowed. Coconut husk fiber is sold by many breeders and pet stores. Many frogs also need a place to hide. Some people use clay pots or fake logs in the terrariums. Fake plants made especially for reptile and amphibian terrariums can also be used. These plastic plants are better than live plants because you can clean them easily and you do not have to worry that the

Leaping Frogs

All frog terrariums or tanks need a secure screen on top to prevent your pet from leaping out. It is not safe for your frog to leap around the house loose. There are many dangers to a frog that could lead to injury or even death. Also, the frog could make your other pets sick if they pick the frog up in their mouths. You must make sure that the cover to your terrarium is either made of screen or has enough air holes so that your frog can breathe easily.

plants are poisonous to your frog. Pet stores often have the supplies to turn a regular terrarium into the perfect environment for your frog friend.

Cleanliness is very important whenever you keep any kind of pet. Your frog's terrarium should be cleaned regularly. This will prevent your frog from getting sick and can also prevent you from getting sick. When you clean out your frog's terrarium be sure to wipe down and wash all the different parts. Never clean your frog's terrarium in your kitchen or bathroom sink, since frog germs can make you sick. If you use your tub or another sink to wash the terrarium, make sure an adult uses strong cleaning detergents to scrub the area afterward. Always wash your hands and arms with soap and water after cleaning your frog's terrarium.

Temperature

Frogs and other amphibians are **cold-blooded** animals. This means that their body temperatures are determined by their environment. (Warm-blooded animals, like humans, dogs, and birds, have body systems that help to regulate body temperature.) Because frogs are cold-blooded, their living space cannot be too hot or too cold. Most frog species do well in temperatures ranging from 65 to 75 degrees Fahrenheit. In hot temperatures, frogs burrow to stay cool. In cold temperatures, frogs become inactive and often will not eat.

To keep your frog's home warm, you can use a special light. Blue or red light can be used to keep your frog's environment warm at night without disturbing your frog with bright light. Fluorescent

Hibernation

Some species of frogs hibernate, or go into a period of decreased activity in which they do not eat or move around much. If your pet frog begins to hibernate, make sure there is enough safe material for your frog to burrow in. Do not force your frog to eat and do not handle your frog. During hibernation, your frog might not molt. This will cause its skin to build up into a tough layer. Below this layer, however, is moist skin that will keep your frog wet, so do not try to help your frog molt. When it is time for your frog to come out of hibernation, it will molt its skin and begin feeding again.

lights work well during the day, and also help your frog get enough vitamin D. A breeder or pet store worker can advise you on the proper lighting for your frog. When setting up any sort of light, however, get the help and approval of an adult. Electric lights can be a fire hazard and must be placed and plugged into safe areas.

Feeding

Many frogs are **carnivorous**, which means they eat meat—usually insects. Common insects for pet frogs include crickets, mealworms, flies, and ants.

Never give your pet frog food that is larger than its mouth. Bigger frogs, like Pacman frogs, can eat large worms.

Some species of frogs also eat shrimp, baby mice, or other small animals. If you want to keep a pet frog, you will need to handle live insects and maybe even small animals in order to keep your pet healthy. Some frogs are cannibalistic, which means they will eat smaller members of their own species. These frogs are best kept in their own terrarium, apart from other frogs.

Breeders and pet stores sell crickets that are specially bred to feed frogs and other pets.

Crickets are common frog food. Most pet shops that sell amphibians also sell crickets. You might also be able to find crickets for sale through the mail or on the Internet. Other people prefer to collect bugs from outside to feed to their frogs. If you do this, make sure the bugs you collect have not been exposed to pesticides or other chemicals that are used on plants. These chemicals stick to the outside of the insects, and can make your frog sick.

Some people feed the crickets a vitamin so that when the frog eats the cricket, those vitamins are passed along to the frog. This is called **gut loading**. Others sprinkle a vitamin powder directly on the crickets or other bugs they feed their frog. When you buy your frog, ask if and when you should give your frog vitamin supplements. Vitamin supplements are usually available at pet stores.

How much and how often you feed your frog depends on its species. A breeder, veterinarian, or pet store worker can give you that information. Your frog may need to eat every day or as infrequently as once a week. Most young frogs need to be fed once per day. When your frog is finished eating, make sure you remove any live food that remains so that it does not go bad and make your pet sick.

Handling Your Frog

A frog should only be picked up when it is necessary to clean its terrarium or to bring it to a vet. It can be stressful to a frog to be handled by humans, and stress can make the frog sick. Some frogs with poison could release their toxins when handled, which can be harmful to people.

If you must handle your pet frog, do so with the help or supervision of an adult. Use both hands to grasp the frog with a firm and gentle grip around its middle. Lift your frog gently and place it down gently in a secure container. If your frog is an aquatic frog, is very small, or is very active, try catching it in a net instead of holding it. Always wash your hands before and after handling your pet frog.

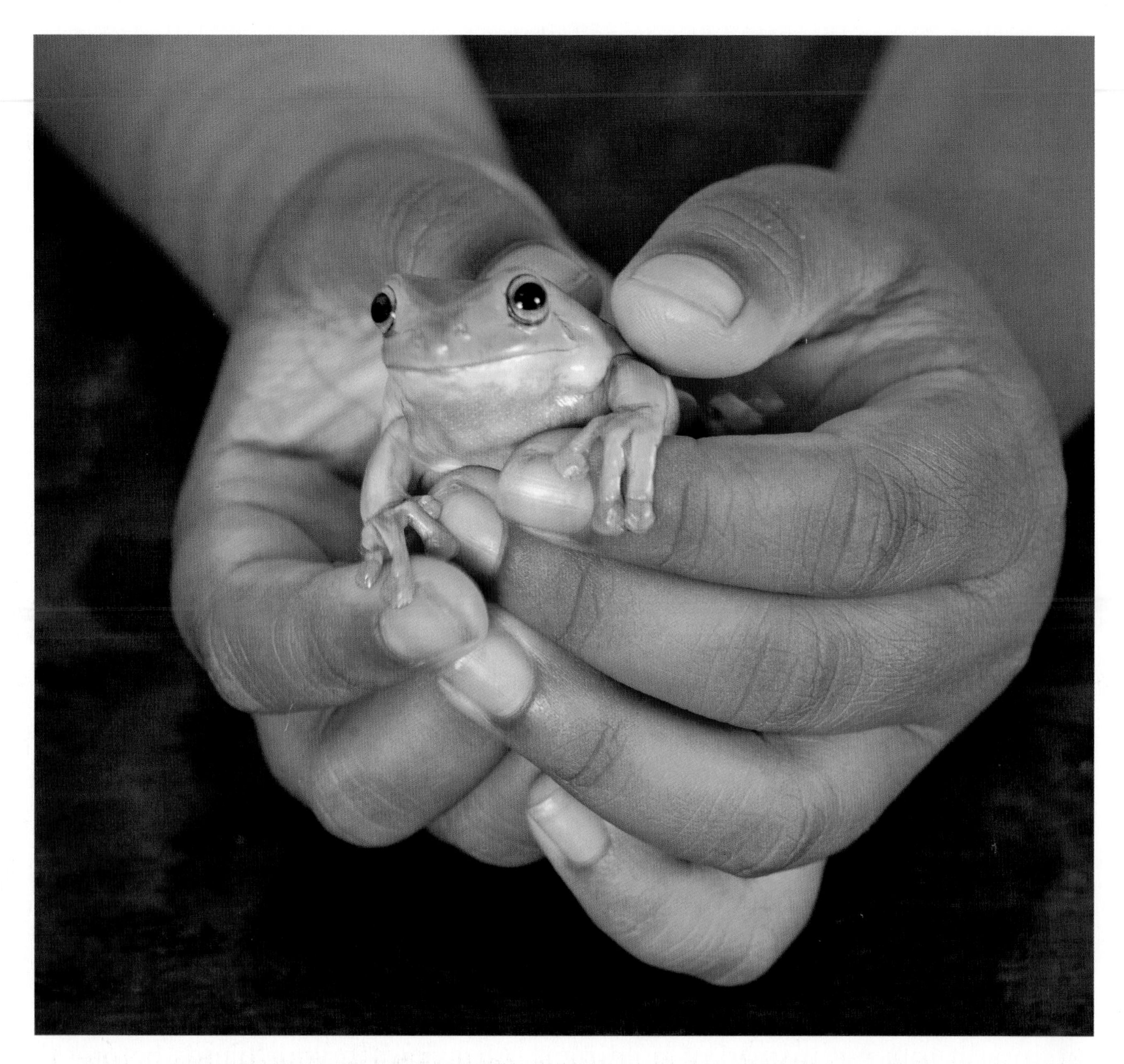

Most frogs do not like to be held and will try to get away from your hands. Always have adult supervision when handling your frog.

Veterinary Care

Like all other pets, frogs may sometimes need the care of a veterinarian, or a vet. This is a special doctor that treats animals. Not all veterinarians treat frogs, so before bringing your frog home find a local vet who specializes in reptiles and amphibians.

Check your frog every now and then to make sure that its skin looks okay and that it does not appear to be hurt or ill.

Unlike dogs, cats, and some other pets, frogs do not need vaccinations or regular medication. But that does not mean frogs never need vet care. If your frog stops eating, seems sick, or has an injury, call your vet and ask if you should bring your pet in.

Frog Diseases

There are a few diseases common to frogs. If you believe your frog might have one of these diseases, bring it to a vet right away.

Red Leg Disease

Red Leg Disease is a sickness that causes the blood vessels in a frog's inner thigh to burst, causing the skin to turn red. The most common cause of this disease is a terrarium with too many frogs and a dirty environment. Other signs of sickness include a loss of appetite, lethargy (when a frog becomes extremely inactive), and weakness. This illness acts very fast, so bring your frog to a vet right away if its legs begin to turn red.

Fungal Infections

When a frog has a cut or another injury to its skin, that area could become infected with fungus. A fungal infection looks white or discolored and could be swollen or red. Your frog's vet can prescribe a treatment in which you soak your frog in a special solution once per day to clear up the fungus.

Metabolic Bone Disease

Metabolic Bone Disese, or MBD for short, is caused by a lack of calcium and vitamin D_3. It can cause your frog to break bones as it hops around. The best prevention for MBD is to make sure your frog has enough calcium and vitamin D_3 in its diet. You can sprinkle your frog's food with a calcium powder or gut load its food. Your frog can get also get vitamin D_3 from a special light over its terrarium. These lights provide special rays that help the skin produce enough of the vitamin for your frog.

Caring for a pet frog can be a lot of work. However, all the work that goes into keeping a pet frog is worth it. Watching it hop around its terrarium, snatching food, croaking out its calls, and soaking in its water can be a lot of fun.

With their interesting looks and behaviors, it is no wonder that many people think that frogs make great pets.

Glossary

amphibians—Cold-blooded vertebrates that live part of their lives on land and part of their lives in water.

aqua-terrarium—An aquarium with a land area and water area.

breeders—People who keep and breed frogs to be sold as pets.

carnivorous—Describes an animal that eats meat.

cold-blooded—A characteristic in which an animal's body temperature is the same as that of their environment.

fertility—The ability to reproduce or support life.

fungus—A type of organism that can grow on an animal and in its environment. Some types of fungus can cause infections and other illnesses in animals and humans.

gills—A body part that allows creatures to breathe underwater.

gut loading—The practice of feeding crickets a vitamin before giving those crickets to a frog. This allows those vitamins to be transmitted to a frog through its food.

hibernate—To become inactive for a period of time, usually during colder temperatures or at certain times of year.

metamorphosis—The transformation of a tadpole into an adult frog.

molt—To shed skin periodically.

predator—An animal that hunts and kills other animals for food.

species—A scientific classification of different types of an animal.

tadpole—An immature frog that looks very different from an adult frog.

terrarium—An enclosure or habitat for a pet, such as a frog or reptile.

toxins—Poisons that cause harm. Some frogs secrete toxins from their skin. Toxins can be deadly or can sometimes cause irritation and illness.

veterinarian—A doctor that treats animals.

vocal sac—A flap of skin under a frog's chin that inflates, or blows up, when noises are made.

Find Out More

Books

Beltz, Ellin. *Frogs: Inside Their Remarkable World.* Ontario: Firefly Books, 2005.

Grenard, Steve. *Frogs and Toads.* Hoboken, NJ: Wiley, 2008.

Mattison, Chris. *300 Frogs: A Visual Reference to Frogs and Toads from Around the World.* Ontario: Firefly Books, 2007.

Moffett, Mark. *Face to Face with Frogs.* Washington, DC: National Geographic Children's Books, 2008.

Websites

Association of Reptilian and Amphibian Veterinarians

http://www.arav.org/USMembers.htm

The ARAV is a group of vets that specialize in treating reptiles and amphibians. Their website has lists of vets who care for frogs and other amphibians and reptiles.

Frogs: A Chorus of Colors

http://www.amnh.org/exhibitions/frogs

The American Museum of Natural History offers this website filled with information about frogs and their evolution and ecosystems. There is also species-specific information, photos, audio files of frog calls, and more.

National Geographic
http://animals.nationalgeographic.com/animals/amphibians.html
This website features detailed information about different frog species, as well as videos, photo galleries, and more.

University of Michigan Museum of Zoology Animal Diversity Web
http://animaldiversity.ummz.umich.edu/site/topics/frogcalls.html
This website has information about and pictures of many different frog species. It also has audio files with the sounds of the different calls of several frog species.

About the Author

Johannah Haney has written about turtles, parrots, ferrets, and small birds for the *Great Pets* series. She has also authored books for young people about endangered animals, health, writing, and social issues. She has a Masters degree in publishing and writing from Emerson College and lives in Boston with her husband and their pets.

Index

Page numbers for illustrations are in **bold.**